The Whetstone

Maura Johnston

SUMMER PALACE PRESS

First published in 2019 by

Summer Palace Press
Cladnageeragh, Kilbeg, Kilcar, County Donegal, Ireland
and
Pegasus
137 Ballantine Gardens, Hillhall Road, Lisburn,
Ballymullan, County Antrim BT27 5FJ

© Maura Johnston

Printed by Nicholson & Bass Ltd.

A catalogue record for this book is available from the British Library

ISBN 978-0-9954529-3-0

This book is printed on elemental chlorine-free paper

for Jack, Helen, Rosie, Catherine and Cillian

Acknowledgements

Some of these poems have been published in: *Candle and Mirror* (Issue 004, 2007); *Pen to Page* (Arts and Cultural Development, Cookstown Council 2010); *moment* (Poetry in Motion 2013); *Washing Windows: Irish Women Write Poetry* (Arlen House 2017); *The Bees' Breakfast* (2017); *Four X Four* (online 2017); *First Seamus Heaney New Writing Award Anthology* (2015). 'The Ballinderry River' was commissioned by the WWF through BREA.

I wish to acknowledge with gratitude the Individual Artist Bursary awarded by the Arts Council of Northern Ireland.

Biographical Note

Maura Johnston was born in Moneymore and after returning from Derry City and Swaziland, has lived there for the past forty-three years. Since her retirement from full-time employment in education, she has worked with children in cross-community projects and on writing projects with a variety of groups. She has compiled two books with schools: for Seamus Heaney on his seventieth birthday, and for the opening of the Seamus Heaney Homeplace. Recently, for Mid Ulster Council, she collated the memories the people of Bellaghy have of Seamus Heaney. She is writer-in-residence at the Palace Stables and at the Navan Centre, Armagh.

She was shortlisted for the Brian Moore Short Story competition and three of her stories were broadcast on BBC Radio Ulster. Her first collection of poetry, *Just Suppose*, was published in 2000.

Contents

My father as a young man	11
My father loved to use words	12
My father wore, depending	13
My father drank three whiskeys	14
My father, five slow days before he died	15
Loss	16
For Patrick	17
As Far as it Goes	
Imbolc	20
Bealtaine	21
Lughnasa	22
Samhain	23
So	24
Campsite near Lubeck	25
Home	26
Neighbourhood Watch	27
The Ballinderry River	28
Beyond the Oak Grove	29
On the Beach	30
The Moss Road	31
Evening in Belfast	32
Reliving	33
The Necessities of Life	34
Afternoon	35
Old Love	36
Disagreement	37

Separation	38
Island Winter	39
Anniversary	40
A Kitchen	41
The Swing	42
Auntie Minnie Comes Home from America	43
Journeying	44
At Granny's House	45
The Keeper	46
I couldn't wait for them to go	47
To Catherine	48
For Cillian	49
The Cellist	50
Tree Music	51
Drumming Match at The Drapers Arms	52
Under the Sky	53
Footsteps	54
Now We Know	55
Trusting	56
Road's End	57
Endings	58
Daddy, you were close to me this June day	59
Alison is Seventy	60
Over	61
Colours	62
New Year's Eve	63
This Is My Time	64

My father as a young man,
six feet tall, with startled hair,
would plough, make hay,
herd cattle on Fair Days.

In the evenings he would meet Eamonn
and Gerry McNaney at the road end
to smoke and laugh his large laugh,
walk the three miles home where,
hearing him come from his *randyvoo*,
the mare in the barn would softly nicker.

My father loved to use words;
called himself *a knight of the road*,
rattled daily to Belfast in his
small, green Bedford lorry (BNT 241)
carrying potatoes to McVeighs
in Mays Market, chugging and shaking
past milestones, missing nothing and
missing everything. Dreaming of making
a stir, himself helmeted, streamlined
on a motor bike, mind blown.
Full Throttle was the name
of his dog-eared book,
the only book he ever owned.

My father wore, depending
on the job in hand, either yellow boots
or wellingtons, which he called waders.

He'd sit on his chair, put
his legs straight out and one of us
would bend and brace and pull,
kneeling for a better grip, face
close to trouser turn-ups, full
of hayseeds, cigarette ash, pig meal.

And when we bumped back and down,
boots in our hands, a grunt
meant *'Thank you, daughter.'*

My father drank three whiskeys
on my sister's wedding day.
Standing, he wept, bewildered,
as she blithely went away.
Later, Guinness in hand, still
brittle in this unused sorrow,
he rallied to his usual high spirits
and took it for what it was worth.

My father, five slow days before he died,
suffered his seventy-sixth birthday
lying in his loosened skin on the sofa.

My mother patted his hand tentatively
and he whispered, *Give us a wee birdie* –
the words he used when we were children
and we'd kiss the stubbly chin or cheek.

I left them then, being neither needed
nor noticed; left them there together,
not touching, bound together. I, feeling
how unknown, unknowable it all was.

He'd have relished, had he known it, *buss*.

Loss

The night I was reintroduced to the dark
was a grace gifted. Light's absence
brought about the birth of peace, for after this loss
nothing, surely, could ever be worse.

For Patrick
1946-2000

Darkness sniffs us out,
lolling in abandonment,
and settles itself.

Language taps down grief.
There's comfort in the silence
we use to point words.

Wine still in the jug,
soda farls buttered, jam spread.
You've fallen asleep.

Pale under asphalt,
creeping under concrete –
ivy and bindweed.

Veins that carry
our heartscald – fuchsia bleeding
in an autumn hedge.

Wild geese, wings brushing
the haunting, helpless moon
with our cobwebbed sleeping.

An evening seething with starlings.
Those uninhibited city birds
at home here in the cut meadow
soaring and swooping and scrabbling heavenwards.

You should have been here too, among friends,
reminding us of other summers
that pulled the hayfield taut about twilight,
funnelling the thran drum's thrum.

Instead we talked of you, and how
you slipped away to open the field –
the skilled scytheman, whetting the blade,
laying low the first untidy swathe
so that in the stinging aftergrass I stood,
an orphaned sister with a lost childhood.

For on a sunny September morning: fields warm, humming;
dahlias vigilant in the garden; terrier for once not busy;
house sound asleep – you sighed,
left your heart in Mowillian,
were flung far from the farm, are a blind wanderer
among ignorant stars where our thin cries
sing sadly, wildly, calling you, calling you –
a startled stranger, a disarmed kerne.

Our heartache swells out at dusk, when sibilant springs
whisper at muddy gaps. Seasons have
congealed to the chill of thorns held in thickets
and a scalded milking tin upended on the hedge.

As Far as it Goes
for James when he was dying

Imbolc
At the end of this short day candles come into their own.
Steady, slight, they waver only when our stories flare out
and with green rushes underfoot we'll imagine
evenings stretching to the farthest shore
and voices chorusing
and we remembering.

Bealtaine
In the hieroglyphs you drew, my name began with an owl
and a mouth. I wanted words of wisdom as we sat
balancing our days, folding away our memories
linen fresh from the hedge
scented with the whitethorn
that ghosts the late spring night.

Lughnasa
Flames leap, Lady assumed into heaven
whatever that means
however she did it
if she did it
your face in the firelight contorts
and you ask
how will I know I am dead?

Samhain
There's a wild wind in the trees tonight
spirits tearing through the mesh of time
freeing us into litanies of being
so put the fat bottle on the table
three swallows, a golden glow
we'll have a rosinner before we go.

So
Seamus Heaney 1939–2013

We take the sky for granted.
Under it we dance in time,
holding hands, holding together,
craning and reading the signs.

We have learned to know the sky,
cloud runes and lightning notes,
white-outs and heat haze,
starling swarm and jet scroll.

We quicken when the wind blows,
tautens the tent of air.

But what desolation when a sudden split
rent that air, tore ties away,
so at the back of our heads,
reflected in dark water,
an immanent universe
ravels in silence.

Campsite near Lubeck

There's nothing like a glass of Rioja for breakfast
with chill German skies holding back the sun
and trees susurrussing along the site
and a black rabbit tethered by a long, green leash
and tzatziki strident on my tongue
and blue plastic bowls holding globules of milk.

And Lubeck beckoning – red brick, black glaze
pushing out of the faraway bombing
back to when Death dances with the traveller,
the workman, even the Pope.

Home

I've heard saxophone music ribbon
from a silk-merchant's house in Lyons.

I've lipped salty, soft pretzels
in Manhattan canyons.

I've seen swans ratcheting their stately way
over the diatomite at Toome.

But nothing can compare to coming home,
home to Mowillian.

Neighbourhood Watch

The factory horn from Cookstown, tinny in the distance,
called my mother from bed at half past seven
to coax the breakfast fire into life.

At half twelve and at half one that same horn
bracketed a time for lunch. And at half five,
quitting time for some, it came to us across the plain,
in the vastness of a summer evening.

When the wind was in the right direction
the Angelus bell could be heard,
dignified, measured, at noon and at six.

George the postman, straight-backed on his bicycle,
arrived regular as clockwork.

No one in our neighbourhood needed a watch.

The Ballinderry River

Camlough, that calm lough, fringed with reeds
lies secret in the quiet hills of Tyrone.
There among cobweb-crocheted whins,
a sudden spring,
a sighing gurgle – the river's begun.

Plaiting and purling, silkily sliding – the water wanders along.
Tinkling and wrinkling, rumbling and tumbling – this is the river's song.

Placid, it passes through Dunamore, ranunculus
drifting over the pearl-musselled gravel bed.
A heron hefts itself into the sky; an otter lithely
insinuates itself into the tangled river weeds.

Plaiting and purling, silkily sliding – the water wanders along.
Tinkling and wrinkling, rumbling and tumbling – this is the river's song.

Wellbrook, and the weight of wheel and weir and years,
curls and whirls in the boulder-buttoned flood.
Hiding speckled trout and snub-nosed dollaghan,
it slips on past Cookstown, cradling salmon parr and smolt.

Plaiting and purling, silkily sliding – the water wanders along.
Tinkling and wrinkling, rumbling and tumbling – this is the river's song.

Below Big Bridge and Coagh Bridge, fishermen cast and hope
and muse as feather, leaf, twig drift lazily past,
twirl into the merging dark Lissan water,
swirl as the river surges through Ballinderry,
under the footgo, into Lough Neagh at last.

Beyond the Oak Grove

The Woods of Killetra and Glenconkeyne
are long since gone.
Loughinsholin is bereft of oak,
birch, hazel and thorn.
Only over Drumlamph ravens still soar,
slide above thorn and ash
where the gash of Glenshane lumbers along
and in an apple-acid autumn evening
stops at the farthest reach
where flat-backed Slieve Gallion,
home to McGarveys, McGreevys,
McCanns and McGuckins
and turf,
hovers at the eye's edge.

And here in the big thicket
we're at home –
Devlins, Donnellys,
McGuiggans, McKees –
on red till and limestone
with quarries and kilns
and trees.

The Barn Yard, the Town Clock,
the Fair Hill, the Assembly Rooms
and trees

with shelter, songs, shadows,
secrets and silence
and the Round Bush
where courting couples met
once upon a time.

On the Beach

Into our sight
come fishermen reeling seaweed
from a disgruntled sea

boy racers ruffle the sand
brake in tandem
in cars too big for them

stutter-stopping short
of an awkward shuffling groom
whose eyes never leave

his bride on a white pony
her swirling skirt
scarlet shoes

a shell on the sand
is curled into a hoof print
and is not broken

and whatever the larks
are up to up there
they are unaware of us

The Moss Road
for Father Raymond Murray

The evening is pleasant,
but swallows are skimming low
– sign of a sad summer –
and under the smooth asphalt
we sense things lurk,
whitened roots, uneven stones,
lacy fossils, bloodied turf.

Those who spread the tar,
the screenings, who rolled it flat
meant it to last,
but didn't understand
our moss roads, their ability
to offer sudden jolts,
belly bumps,
the possibility
of cracks and chasms.

All it takes is one strong soul
to shout to the winds,
to the hungry listeners,
to unpick one corner
leaving the rest to time,
to frost and to the certainty
that the swallows will return.

Evening in Belfast

The sudden rare sunshine
lifts my ready heart to quiver
with whispering new leaves –
low, ear-stretching whispers of *Never! Never!*

What, I think, can never come again?
First love, that began right here
in shuttered streets, in spring sun and in rain,
when we linked hands and held each other near.

That green love has gone, I don't deny,
replaced by something sturdier,
for love, like leaves, can wither and can die –
its absence a cold hollow in a tree.

To keep our love alive we've taken pains;
much has gone, but so much more remains.

Reliving

Don't tell me things.
Don't name them.
I know before you tell me.

That sudden lift of wings –
sea birds declining the shore.

The bone-rattles are reeds,
the beat of our retreat.

The heart is a muscle
that can atrophy if unused.

Jealousy is blind burning
and is for the young.

Tears wash the eyes kindly.
Peace is alone.

Mornings open days.
Afternoons linger.

When thoughts are slippery
in my muddied brain
I'll need you then.

The Necessities of Life

When I think of what I need
you top the list.

Forget breathing or eating
– or at least we'll assume
breathing and eating.

You could, if you would, fill my world.

Afternoon

What is this persistence in your pleading
asking me of love in our afternoon?
Casual love, tending to tedium
for time has worn the blossom and the bloom.

Think October morning, simple sunlight
complacent on frost-angled walls and roofs
as well-fed uncles' wide embroidered smiles
recall past pleasures of spirited youth.

Think of familiar music changing tenor,
threading the keening fiddle through the flute,
pulling our sung solo songs together
like whangs that tighten weather-beaten boots.

Think of memories and measured passion;
it is our evening now, not afternoon.

Old Love

When I hear the pock, pock of a snail shell
knocked by a hopeful thrush upon a stone,
or see you trace the fluting of a bird bone
I sense the hidden things that you don't tell:
soul secrets, deep as water and as still.
I'll dowse for them with wiles I've made my own,
and pull them to the surface one by one,
caressing to alleviate their chill.

So come now, tell me soft that all is well;
we still can tread a measure eye to eye
and learn with certainty to read one sign
of a finite eternity – the bell,
flinging its tongue in brazen symmetry
around the broken syllables of time.

Disagreement

Last night we disagreed.
It was, you might say, a storm;
gales shaking our house and cold
air puffing through cracks. No harm
was done to any living creature.
And yet who is to say what
ridges have corrugated my heart
or yours in the aftermath where
we are tensed, flensed, flayed.

Separation

The swinging fuchsia
curtains the cracks in the wall
that keeps me from you.

This cold night, silence,
like wet flannel, muffles
the sighs of lonely hearts.

In moonlight the lane,
a fall of silver, frozen
distance between us.

In the icy night
your footsteps pad to my door.
Your hand hesitates.

The knife-edge of dawn
brings only sorrow to me
with the pain of light.

The underbellies of clouds
press relentlessly onto
hollows in my hopes.

Over the nettles
the light creeps
towards a smoulder
of wall-hugging ivy.

Island Winter

Last night cold air sidled under the door and lingered.
All day, wind had thrummed on the rusty wire fence
and rattled through, pachled through, dried broken reeds.

You remembered your grandfather in the Depression years
taking his young family on holiday to a house like this
and waving burning turf on the tongs to share the scent.

Tonight we've moved side by side closer to the fire,
to sparking driftwood and the whuff of falling turf ash.

Now whatever roams outside, pads outside our warmth.
We cradle hot whiskeys, sealed and settled in.

Anniversary

I took you a bowl of cherries
a small bowl of cherries
almost past their best
some wrinkled
enough were plumply ripe
so that juice ran unchecked
over your fingers
and I almost licked it off

A Kitchen

A cat slumbering in the sunlight.
Cupboards keeping their secrets.

In here all is warm as a cinnamon bun,
brown as the crunch of ginger biscuits.

Sunshine pools on the tiles,
strikes notes from the edge of the stirabout pot.

Like a contented cat the kettle purrs
and bubbles, plumping and puffing on the range.

Honey, scented with clover and orange blossom
slopes off the spoon to sweeten another morning.

In the big blue bowl
a scented peach delights the air.

Brown eggs nestle warmly.
My mother's delft is on the dresser.

Somewhere, children crowd and jostle
laughing silently.
I know they're there.
If I turn quickly
surely I will see them.

The Swing

It was a rough rope
that made our swing.
It needed a folded
cushion for padding.

That hairy rope grazed
hands that gripped,
tight-knuckled as
we bucked and tipped
and swung out over
nettles and stones,
knowing one fall
was enough to break our bones.

Still we swung, entering
and leaving air
that sluiced our limbs,
buoyant in an element not ours.

Auntie Minnie Comes Home from America

My hand reaches out for hers
and falls
as her hands, clawed, yellowed,
tug at the sheets' frayed edges, and are never still.

These are the hands that sewed for me – frocks,
First Communion dress, even, once, a coat.

The voice that tried to peel away my accent, slips upward
to fling outrage and obscenity in the squeamish room.

She calls in agitation for the children to come in,
to come for their dinner, to come in from the cold,
oh, why won't they come?

Slats of sunlight bar the wall and her fingers
tremble as she reaches for the light.

Journeying

Maggie Malone read fortunes.
Her thimble was trim on the china
as she turned the tinkling cups
upside down on their saucers.
My aunts tossed back the last drops.

She turned each cup lovingly,
staring in and muttering and clearing her throat.
Look, she'd say, *a letter is on its way,*
I hope the news is good.
And a stranger is coming, a man
by the look of it. Who could that be?
And there's a cat, no maybe a dog.
That bird's a warning.
And the aeroplane means a journey.

She'd peer through her spectacles
and my aunts would shake themselves,
collect the dreamtime dishes
and dump them in the jawtub.

At Granny's House

A brass tap on the front of the range –
little gold snout, smoothly inviting.
I'll just touch it, stroke it,
maybe turn it a little.

My sandals slip slap on the tiles.
I hum.
I reach out.
Get away from there!

I jerk back, scared into silence.
I stare into the corner.
It must be an ogre.

Only my granda, moustache frothed
with the tea he slurps from a saucer,
Sit down, wee girl, or you'll get scalded!

The Keeper

She was the keeper of the candle flame
the darner of dreams that wore thin
the game where he made the rules
the shout of seeping silence
the song in sweet cracked key
the prayer that was ash in the chimney
the laughter that ran with tears
the gleam in dark-forested days
the owl in the blood of the bat-night
the light that shone 'til the end.

I couldn't wait for them to go. We had just had an uncomfortable meal. The food had been fine, steak and chips, salty vinegary chips, food we were unused to, a treat. The discomfort had been among ourselves, thrown into a strange situation: red formica-topped tables; electric lights; city accents. A jukebox played the Stones: *It's all over now*. It was at once too noisy and too private for any normal conversation. We certainly did not mention what was uppermost in our minds. My father ate steadily and drank the hot tea to the dregs, although he complained, to us, that it was too weak. My mother said little and what she did say was in the form of questions. What time had I to be there? Had I remembered my prayer book and rosary beads? Would I send Granny a letter when I had settled? Had I my birth certificate with me?

Now we had arrived. They helped me carry the suitcases into the hallway. I could see my father take in the height of the ceilings, the panelling, the shiny floors, just as he had sat for a long time after he had stopped the car to gaze at the outside of the old building. My mother could not see very much. There were tears in her eyes and she kept her lips firmly closed. Her gloved hands writhed. I knew she found the heady scent of lavender and the heavy silence unnerving. 'Thank you,' I said, 'for everything.' And they went.

I stood in the doorway as they drove off and I wondered if I should have kissed them. When I turned back in I was thinking of the gifts the aunts and neighbours had given me. I thought of electric light and reading in bed. A clock ticked. Who would share a room with me? Mother Isidore came round the corner, hand extended. Before I moved towards her I had time to wonder if this flatness was what freedom felt like.

To Catherine

You race up and down the cot
pointing, babbling
watermelon smile
splitting your face,

that smile that pulls my throat
tight as the top of a bag
of marbles. You poke your fingers
through the bars, catch mine, laugh.

I hoist you out and you latch onto
my haunch and my heart, leaning in
to settle, a demanding little burden
fierce and unyielding
recalling old and weary weights:

a leather bag bursting with learning
bowing my reluctant back;
the drudge and drag of
buckets of well-water; lifting lumps of hay;
the stone of remorse that
ground my sore soul into flitters.

These I cast off, kick, flatten
into Frisbees that bear all hurt away
to leave lightness in their wake.

So tell me why, when we stop our play
and you go on your own sweet way
I suffer a strange and heavy emptiness,
awe-full as world's woe, terrible in its loneliness?

For Cillian

You came the year house martins returned.

Such secret, long, life-driven journeys;
such trust in the enlivening air;
such darting forays into learning.

Laughing, *you* make bold bids for freedom.

Our arms that could outstretch
hesitate to impede your tempestuous flight;
love and wisdom telling us to wait.

And, nestling, when you seek us, you'll find us
under the flight path of raucous autumn rooks.

The Cellist
for Neil Martin

When you lift the bow
your face closes as the day's
eye does at dewfall.

Conjured by the air you coax,
your hands, your sure fingers
moving, touching,

we, exposed, are pierced
through the skin to delight
and sit unsettled.

Tree Music
for David Keys

The flash of ash
in this bone-bare winter hedge
is in pitch-perfect key.

Birch bark tatters
flutter, fan-dancers
to a rag-time rhythm.

In the centre
the fairy thorn jigs in time
to a wayward wind.

And the willow droops
wind-whipped, cross-limbed, swaying
in a soft-shoe shuffle.

Drumming Match at The Drapers Arms
for Eric McKee

The beat
the bones of the beat
find the bones of the roll as the bamboo beats the skin
draws out the beat
beats out the roll
thrums out the roll
and the knuckle-knocking, bamboo-flicking, belly-bearing beat
rolls through the sun-slanted evening
the bones of the beat
find the bones of the roll as the bamboo beats the skin
thrums through the tightened air
and the slanting sun strikes the colours on the drums
the drums
the brattle and the rattle and the roll and the beat
and the drummer's stately strut
and the bones of the beat
find the soul of the roll as the bamboo beats the skin
beats out the roll
draws out the beat
thrums out the roll
and the knuckle-knocking, bamboo-flicking, belly-bearing beat
rolls through the sun-slanted evening
the bones of the beat find the bones of the roll as the bamboo beats the skin
thrums through the tightened air
and the slanting sun strikes the colours on the drums
the drums
the brattle and the rattle and the roll and the beat
and the drummer's stately strut
and the bones of the beat
find the soul of the roll as the bamboo beats the skin
beats out the roll
stops!

Under the Sky

The wide clear grey sky
was swept clean by the freshening wind
that brushed the pelt of wayward grasses
that islanded the house
that contained the rage
that simmered under
the clear grey sky.

Under the roof
birds chastened the attic air
their clawing heard below
like bare feet on broken biscuits
feet tracing old patterns
feet breaking old patterns
feet drawn to the door
to be caught in the whorls
of wind-blown wayward grass.

When lightning whitened the broken shutters
walls split and love fell out.
Catch it before the grasses grow over it
or pull the chocolate soft centre out or
pull the curved smoothness from the rose or
pull the inarticulate hope from sentimental verse.

Catch it, I say, catch it –
love that is wide as a clear grey sky,
as lonely as the silence of clouds of distant geese
going home, going home.

Footsteps

follow me down the street
where dead leaves slap on concrete.
In a soft smirr of rain
I watch my feet
watch my step
find myself walking in time
to the beat of those feet
slapping on pavements
slipping on dead leaves.

I turn my wet face,
search for stars among the rooftops
while my feet keep on padding
on the darkening leaves.

Footsteps
tap echoes back
to catch in the lamplight
like broken words,
dance into my yesterday
with the beat of certainty
and nothing of my frailty.

Now We Know

I was at my desk; the headmaster came in –

when
I heard it
he heard it
we heard it –
skies breaking
seas lurching
paths tilting

I didn't know
he didn't know
we didn't know
what darkness was
what pain was
what emptiness was
'til then –

'til darkness seeped into us
'til pain froze in frosty flowers
'til emptiness was our tomorrow, our forever.

Then I knew
then he knew
then we knew
a new world that opened.

Trusting

The click of the dice, the sighs,
the risks taken over the years
with confidence that flared or fell
like waves splattering a pier.

Did we need to trust in gods,
their moods kind or capricious?

I think we made our own luck,
treating them all with suspicion,
noting magpies, mayflowers, new moons,
rainbows and lonely thorn trees,
tea leaves, rabbit feet, runes.

Road's End

The grey road stops at the sea
that rocks the Island of the Dead
where the unclaimed and the unbaptised
are abandoned to a gull-harsh rest,
restless as those rocking waves,
quiet as the hush of evening.

Endings

It was a shock
when the motor cyclist called out,
Hit the hedge, Grandma!

> *So you haven't seen*
> *the way the road has taken*
> *or its final twist.*

You've gone further, know
more; I've put down spreading roots
that will hurt to tear.

> *I said I'd hug you*
> *but my arms aren't long enough*
> *to circle your dreams.*

Dreams tear too. Mithra
will judge their truth, balancing
fitness and failure.

> *As death approaches*
> *these things don't matter.*
> *The Lord will know his own.*

Daddy, you were close to me this June day.
I sat on the black bare marble surround
of your bed of thirty years, listened for
that hearty loud, loud laugh, felt you confined.
I talked to you, spoke about the weather.
It's a right good day for the hay, I said.
And so it was, warm and dry. A freakish wind,
bruised with mown-grass scents, fluttered, swayed,
blew me back to Buttony and the Front Field.
You could fairly handle a wooden rake,
twist, spin out a grass rope, make all secure.
All gone now, gone the way of the corncrake.
The nights are silent. Today you were quiet
in the careless sunshine. I left you to sleep tight.

Alison is Seventy

Long ago when our beach fire spat at the dark
we baked potatoes.
The boys drank stout
and we, islanded, felt safe.

Now we can discern an edge to the sea's simper,
know that potato skins burn
as keenly as the kisses of those broken boys.

We are stranded above youth's tideline,
our scars proudly borne.
We know what fearless is:
flying alone above the star-tipped waves.

Over
for Mary Crooks

When the party's over the lights are dimmed
and we drift unsteadily away,
an absence hurts and hollows the heart
for all that the brain can say.

Because the one who made the journey light
who led over stony ground
who found something to praise in our stumbling steps
will no longer be around.

The chairs are stacked and the floor swept smooth
our notebooks are closed with care.
We take a last look at the place where we laughed.
We'd wave, but there's no one there.

Colours

I was a novice.

In the dark scriptorium
I learned my colours.

I saw scarlet eat
the tender heart of roses
choking on the blood.

Yellow's sweetness was
honey and sang the blackbird's
fierce heart-drilling song.

Green grew everywhere;
nettle, willow, moss and mint,
lichen-covered bark.

Blue smelled of turf smoke
and fell flatly on the page:
sky-reflecting sea.

And black was absence;
smear of soot; a starless night;
a bottomless well.

New Year's Eve

The evening hardened: early dark
with a clean smell of snow.
Our feet pattered on the pavement.
Year's end, a letting go.

Your muted lamplight invited us,
a glimpse of firelight
and a jug of hopeful white hyancinths
that lit the needy night.

This Is My Time

This is where I am,
in the heartsore loneliness of evening,
and the beauty it brings:

grey-shadowed water;
querulous birds quibbling over nests;
lights in other houses.

And here I am
on the edge of it all,
sensing the coming darkness.

For in darkness it is so easy to lose sense.
Outstretched hands reach through unfeeling air.
Eyes struggle and ears strain.

If lightning should freeze the darkness
into bright antlers, jazz bursts, slivers of jaggedness,
I could, for that second, ground myself.

But here I am
in the half light
knowing and feeling my place

wondering and waiting
for the shy, sharp evening star.
I am here.